Inside My Perceptions

Misty Fletcher

BookLeaf Publishing

Presentation by *BookLeaf Publishing*

Web: www.bookleafpub.com

E-mail: info@bookleafpub.com

ISBN: 9789395950978

First edition 2022

I dedicate my work to my daughter Adyson.
May she know dreams are what we make
them to be, regardless of how big or small.
She is my heart and my purpose.

ACKNOWLEDGEMENT

I thank God for the trials, tribulations, and lessons that inspired me to be all that He created me to be.

I thank my friends and family that have supported me relentlessly and pushed me to be the best version of myself.

PREFACE

Here lies the pieces of my heart that have been battered, broken, and healed. These are the innermost thoughts of a lover, mother, daughter, sister, addict, and friend.

Poetry is my passion. It's the one thing that has always been there for me; my outlet. My goal is to be vulnerable and transparent so that my readers are able to connect and relate on some level.

My hope is evoke emotion through the power of words.

Lost Until Found

I was young and naive,
When the world grabbed a hold of me.

Promiscuous.

Was it love or lust?
Misplacing trust, left in the dust.
Mistakes, heartbreaks, I'd never learn.
Kept getting burned,
Until it was my turn to cause the hurt.
I took the shame and let it reign.

Material possessions became an unhappy lesson.
Chemical obsessions led to unsavory
confessions.
I was lost in my empty oppression.
Self made prison, battling with no vision, in
need of wisdom.

Scared and alone, no place to call home.
Death seemed to be the answer.
Abducted by my demons with no ransom.

Years wasted running from reality.
Somehow constantly escaping fatality,

Until truth hit me in the face.
Such a brutal and bitter taste.
No chance of winning the endless race.
Time to leave the past without a trace.

Choices led to change.
Surrender gave God an open range.
Finally came in out of the pouring rain.
Growth continues everyday.
A promise to never give in to my old ways.

Twisted Desire

The night summons like an unquenched love
beckoning with the promise of dark desire.
An insatiable need that burns for a touch that can
only be harvested in the most unlikely of places.

There you are, I see your face.
I see you behind a facade of only what you want
to allow.
There's a difference in seeing and believing, I
know that now.

A mysterious entity lurks in your shadow that
has only been cast upon me,
because that's how you want it to be.

I thirst for that passion and drink up all that
you'll give.
Like a drug I want more; drunk on lust.

I want you.
I need you.
It is a must.

Falling fast into a trap of endless sexuality.
There is a difference between fantasy and reality.

Why do we proceed into a path marked tragic?
You next to me, we make magic.

There is perfection intertwined into the
provocative affairs of the heart.

Always running from the pain, but what feels
good is elusive.
When we catch feelings, the heart is intrusive.

Is my heart beating to be involved or are the
body's urges so strong illusions cloud what is
real?

How do you do this? You make me feel.

What I see behind your eyes tells a different
story than your mouth can say.
Curiosity brings about notions of "what if"and
they take me away.

Night drifts and I awake from a dream that was
so tangible, my body aches for that touch.
A craving that hurts so GOOD, I want it so
damn much.

So decadent and delicious, the possibility to live
without becomes too much to perceive.
I want to hold on, I want to believe.

The burden of that loss is so powerful that
surrender to its temptation is explosive.
The ice around my heart is erosive.
Full of orgasmic relief, a lifetime of tension
simultaneously combusts.

The line between fantasy and reality is distorted.
Can my heart afford it?

Cozy

Lying in an endless cloud of pillows and
blankets, all wrapped up in you.
No words, yet the room is overflowing with
passion.
You take my breath away.
The look in your eyes says you want me; that
you see only me.
Your breath on my skin, tell me where have you
been?
The taste of your kiss reminds me of home, to
the place I want to go.
Hopeless romantics starving for each other's
touch.

Can't you see, it's always been you?
Time stands still, for a moment it's just us.
This is where we belong.
Being next to you is a rush.
You are the poetry in my soul and the music that
makes me melt.
My inspiration, my frustration.
Come closer and never let go.
Let love live here, let it grow.

Undefined Love

We walk through our lives wandering.
Making choices and decisions.
Living with the consequences of sliding doors
and silver linings;
the "what if's" and "could have been's".

WHAT IF WE LET ALL THAT GO?

Stale bitterness, resentment and revenge bring
the soul to a place of solitude and misery.

WHY BE THAT WAY?

Instead, live in a place; a state of mind, that
encourages the inner being to rush freely; to run
wild through a field of dreams that won't decay.
Let them thrive like the sound of your heart
beating as you fall in love.
Recognize this could be an opportunity to unify.
Realize the heart beats differently when it's not
broken.
When it's healing it begins feeling some warmth,
a glimpse of hope.
It's terrifying yet exhilarating at the same damn
time.

Optimism plants seeds that when nourished trust grows.

When fertilized and watered it flourishes into a magnificent, natural masterpiece.

It's vulnerable and fragile, but in the right hands, in the correct environment, LOVE grows.

It becomes its own living entity that can wither without warmth and care, but will evolve into the most extraordinary result NEVER imagined.

A force to be reckoned with.

A triumph that cannot be defeated by the past haunting.

It overpowers the pain and heals what is broken.

It liberates, it sets free.

It's undefined love that's yet to be.

It's an equation awaiting a solution.

It's simplicity of words of wisdom set free.

Undefined love, just let it be.

Adyson

My little girl with bright eyes, you give me the
world.
You give me reason to sustain this life I thought
wasn't worth living.
Your laugh illuminates my soul.
You fill a place where pain left an empty hole.
My girl, forever saving me.
Mommy is the name I'll always keep.
You shape me into the person God intended me
to be.
One day you'll see.
I watch you as you sleep, embracing the only
love that could ever run this deep.
This bond I cherish and keep.

Baby girl, you are my priority.
I'm here to talk, laugh, and listen.
I accept, guide, and watch you glisten.
Your tears I'll wipe, kiss your fears goodbye.
No matter what mommy is by your side.
Couldn't push me away even if you tried.
The best thing that has ever happened to me,
when you have your own baby you'll see.
Know you can be anything.
Give your all. That's what you'll have to bring.

This world can be cold and cruel.
Let your heart be your living fuel.
Stay true to yourself, baby don't succumb.
Then you'll thrive and love all you become.
Mommy is here to hold your perfect hand.
I'll hold you up when you are too scared to stand.
Tomorrow is on the horizon, you'll forever be my shimmering diamond.

Into the Deep

On the surface you see what it is she wants you
to see, a sparkling smile with confidence that
brightens a room.
A delicate flower attracted to the sun, exuding
brilliant colors of life.
Beauty that lies on the surface, but lacking
strength to withstand harsh winters.

It's easier that way, for you to think she is not
complicated, only in need of the simplicity of
life's necessities.
Deep within she needs nutrients to help her
thrive, to encourage the brilliance of her blooms.

Beyond what you can see are deep roots that
keep her grounded, bound to the essence of her
camouflaged realities.
Only authenticity can see past what human eyes
are capable of viewing.

Behind her eyes lives a story only few can
comprehend and she craves their presence.
The complexities of her mind and heart long for
a deeper connection.

She has settled for solitude because there she feels safe and free to just be.
No longer controlled or forced to pretend to be who it is you want her to be.
Here it has become less challenging to let go of the fight to truly be seen.

She has found realization that loneliness is abundant in a crowded space and true intimacy is a rare occurrence.
There is such value in what is genuine and organic; such relief found when there is at least one who can feel her truth without a word spoken.

Inhale fresh purpose and exhale false indoctrination.

She says goodbye to her chameleon attributes and welcomes her bold uniqueness that pushes her out of the crowd.

She'll never float on the surface again. She's into the deep.

What pushes you out of the crowd? It is time to take that leap.

Nostalgia

If I could choose a time, if I could press rewind,
I'd go back to a day when life had a simpler way.
Last day of school skipping class;
Running barefoot in the grass;
Family camping at the lake;
Not realizing the memories we'd take.
Lightning bugs were the magic of night.
Playing hide and seek with no flashlight.
The smell of honeysuckle in summer air is the
fragrance of life with no cares.
Cassette tapes and VCRs;
Not wearing seatbelts in the car.
Summer crush and bikinis;
Saved By The Bell and Mr. Feeney;
Roller skates and bike rides;
Beach trips and changing tides;
Sneak out the window to say we could;
Knowing every trail in the woods,
Being outside for hours,
Never worried about sick prowlers.
Take me back to that place, life was lived at a
different pace.
A time when devices didn't rule the days;
Imagination blossomed and paved the way.

If we only knew the good ole days were in those moments, we would have embraced, loved, and owned it.
Lessons learned for us to teach,
Cherish right now before it's just a memory out of reach.

Light Overcomes

For so long I dwelled in a dumpster of fear.
When I would climb out, I carried the stench of
regret.
I relished the stink, because it kept people at a
distance.
The further away, the less they could hurt me.
I craved solitude, sought out silence.
Snuff out sound and light.
Darkness was my friend.
Death was knocking on my door, but I couldn't
grasp why the beast never carried me across the
threshold.
He taunted me.
He lured me in with promises of silent darkness
that would forever hold me.
In my comfortably numb state of being, a
piercing light penetrated my icy forcefield.
Light kept stinging my presence, waking me up
from my slumber.
I wanted to give up, stab it with a steely knife
but I couldn't kill the beast.
I began moving closer to the light and shadows
dissipated.
Tears helplessly fell.

There was a face in the mirror staring back at me.
Abused and broken, by her own hands.
Self sabotage.
Nowhere to go, nowhere to run, I fell to my knees.
Suddenly, as I cried out for help, I heard a subtle whisper of truth.
"Misery and despair were the treacherous outcomes of the choices made. You can choose something new"
My spirit crushed, I crumbled to the floor.
An unfamiliar warmth permeated my soul, it encapsulated my being and coddled my mind.
As thoughts slowed from their constant race, surprisingly I knew I had a choice to make.
A soothing guide from an unseen hand showed me where to go.

In darkness the light is most feared.
Light restores and relinquishes control that darkness hides.
Truth is light and it liberates.
The lies hold captive and bore prisoners of pain.
Pain dwells in a dumpster of fear keeping truth away.
Isolation breeds devastation and lives swirl the drain.

Let the light shine and heal the hurt that is
hiding in the darkest crevices of your soul. There
is a Savior, He is Truth and Light.

Vodka Filled Tears

I just wanted you to hold my hand; to hold my
hand when it would really count.
Stop looking back, put the bottle down, and hold
my hand.
Many moons have passed, but there was
something we couldn't grasp.
We knew how to laugh.
We knew how to cry.
We danced between the sheets, but you could
not look me in the eyes.
You mastered the lies.
After all these years, after all my fears you kept
running back to vodka filled tears.
She took your soul and made you hers, now
we're living under vodka's curse.
Empty bottles replaced your empty heart.
That little girl lives with all our hurt.
I just can't understand why she can't come first.
God can quench your thirst if you'd surrender
and put Him first.
Instead we lived with vodka filled tears.
You had this smile, you had this wit, you had
these smarts, but you just won't quit.
It's liquid danger that took my man and made
him a stranger.

Now I walk alone with emptiness in my hand,
for my little girl I had to make a final stand.
I've grown weary from seeing her cry vodka
filled tears, to save her from this curse for all her
years.
Aren't you tired of playing with fire, when will
you let go of your liquid desire?
I could never compete with that heat.
80 proof is the company you keep.
How does it feel watching your family walk
away?
Did you know I always wanted to stay?
I just couldn't keep crying vodka filled tears.
After all these years, vodka consumed my
reluctant fears.
Days turned to night, a decade washed away.
In the silence of your pain, only God can change
the way.

Reckless

Reckless.
I have been reckless.
I jumped in going nowhere fast, staring in the
rearview, romancing the past.
Emotions running high, like teardrops from the
sky.
Believing all the lies.
Failure, too many tries.

Reckless, emotionally reckless.

Wearing my heart on my sleeve, thieves of the
night, takes it and leaves.
Down on the floor, pleading on my knees, "God
take this pain away from me!
I know I cannot do this alone, so please, take
this pain away from me!"

I'm reckless, emotionally reckless.

My heart is in distress, drunk on the look in your
eyes.
Falling in love with you was my bitter demise.
Every night filled with tear drenched cries.

I was never enough for you to stay, no matter
what you pushed me away.

Go away and leave me alone, after all the
disrespect that you've shown.
The pathetic truth is, if you come knocking on
my door, I'll accept you back for more, because

I'm reckless, emotionally reckless.

If you love me please stay gone.
My heart cannot take this off and on.
You've broken me down so many times, the way
you hurt me should be a crime.
I want you to feel the pain you inflicted.
To the chaos, I became addicted. Withdrawing
from your touch.
I missed it way too much.

I'm reckless, emotionally reckless.

I can't trust myself to walk away.
My heart will only lead me astray.
I fear not having you near.
My soul you crushed, you got to go, it's a must.
Now I have misplaced trust.
Was it love or lust?
Like a drug I couldn't get enough. I want you
too damn much.

Leave me to just be me.
Alone with my thoughts, to remember how we
fought; how you left me to rot.
Did you even love me or not?
I hate that I even have to ask.
It doesn't matter you need to stay in my past.
I am twisting and turning.
My soul is on fire, it's burning.

I reckless, emotionally reckless.

Soon I'll be heartless, hardened and jaded, bitter
and faded.

You created this mess but I must confess,
Your power over me is gone.
You thought you'd win, but you are very wrong.
Too late, I've moved on.
That is enough of this heartbreak song.
You can't put out my fire.
This game you lost, it's time to retire.
Try me and you'll see, it's your turn to be on
your knees.
Beg and plead.
You've lost me, because you're

Reckless, emotionally reckless.

You played a game you thought you would win.

Truth is, I'm over you and that toxic grin.

Together we are reckless, emotionally reckless.

No longer forever, the damage is done.

It's reckless, emotionally reckless.

Symphony In My Heart

It takes me away to another place.
I can recall the smell and remember the taste.
The emotions.
The vibrations.
The energy.
Who I was and who I wanted to be.
The sound, all around.
The beat has me tapping my feet.
Moving my hips to words coming off my lips.
The resonance.
The way we dance.
Music is the magic in my soul.
It's the symphony in my heart.
Rhythmic art.
It's timeless harmony that lives in my memory.
The soundtrack of my life, holds the power to
change the vibe.
Iconic.
Ironic.
Semi-sonic.
Exotic and we rock it.
When it plays, I start to sway.
In the moment I can stay.
Takes me back in time, I can press rewind with
the rhythm and the rhyme.

The symphony in my heart.
Rhythmic art.
Collaborative sounds moving through the air,
lifting my cares.
Woodwind.
Piano.
Strings.
Percussion.
Poetry given a beat, now it's fun.
Lyrical masterpiece.
Gives my ears a musical feast.
Each new song is a sensory treat.
A symphony stored in my heart.
Rhythmic art.
A gift.
A treasure.
A fantasy of different measure.

Dear Trauma

You came into my life when I was broken.
I was shut off, distant, never open.
You kept hoping.
Time went on, patience morphed into frustration.
In your eyes, time was wasting.
Somewhere in between we found heated
jealousy.
Passion grew into control.
I became your object to own.
I lost my soul.
Caught up in your lover's cage.
I felt all your rage.
In your mind, I was to blame.
You lifted me higher than I'd ever known, but I
landed in my darkest lows.
You taught me what love was by showing me
what it wasn't.
I got lost deep in your eyes, but in the end it was
me you despised.

Insecurity, jealousy, and sexual greed.
Obsessions of the mind.
Threats of you leaving me dead for them to find.
What I wanted to say you'll never know.
I put a smile on my face so nobody would know.

Too scared to be real.
Constantly questioning how you'd feel.
You wanted someone I could never be.
I lost who I was until I was no longer me.
The shoes you wanted me to wear would never fit.
I was just molding clay in your girlfriend starter kit.
I was bent and shaped, twisted and baked.
I was yours to make.
Still I couldn't get it right.
Slowly you put out my shining light.

You wore rage like a smoking gun.
Fear was my pass time, too scared to run.
Lies told a haunted tale until tragedy fell.
I was without your instruction.
I didn't know how to function.
Downward spiral of self destruction.
I had to find the path back to me.
You never wanted that, now I see.

Discontent Troubled Waters

There have been so many times when I was
ready for this life to pass me by.
Tears falling as I mourned the years.
Somehow I was caught up in a place I'd never
been, a face I'd never seen, a song I'd never
sang.
Never satisfied.
Always searching and hurting for something that
never was, and never would be.

It was all made up.
Fabricated by a day dreamer.
Eyes fixated on a sun that would never set.
The girl that laughed in the face of fear, only to
find fear is what consumed her.

There is freedom in letting go of that self made
prison; the one that locks you in your own mind.
An endless search for something more, but you'll
never find.
A trap of not good enough and wanting better.
The face in the mirror disgusted by the judges
behind the online screen.

Still being graded by self-appointed teachers
with no real education other than fake news and
social media posts.
What a joke.
I long to know more, to have understanding but
at the core harboring a need to be understood.

Most alive in the deepest waters because I
drown in surface level insignificance.
I find home in solitude, yet crave the presence of
one that sees through the darkness into the light
of me.
The light I couldn't see.

A turbulent under current pulls from beneath but
is calmed by understanding.
There is truth in the realization that I know
nothing and there is much more than what meets
the eye.

Empath as a Friend

I can feel your pain.
I see the hurt in your eyes.
It's in the way you move.
The energy doesn't lie.
No need to try.
No need to say "I'm ok."
I'm your friend, I won't go away.

I can offer a safe place to breathe.
Exhale the rage.
I promise it will help you turn the page.

I know people let you down.
Trust has a scary sound.
Betrayal is what you've found.
You see, there is something in you that I
recognize in me too.
You'll wipe my tears as they fall, without
judgment or question.
If you give me the chance, I'll reciprocate that
friendship dance.
You'll never need to hide.
Life's been hard for me too, so lets try.
So happy to meet you here.

Little by little we'll let go of our fears.
Build something strong for the coming years.

Addiction

It came in the form of a solution, only to birth a
monsoon of delusion.
It makes promises of great feeling, but in the end
just keeps stealing.
It robs dreams, rips away at the seams.

It will leave you begging for more, crying,
broke, but pleading at their door.

This sick affair starts as innocent fun but wreaks
havoc, wishing you would have run.
Broken homes, shattered dreams, fractured
reality.
A living nightmare is what it seems.
In a place where hope lived, now only shame
exists.
It holds souls prisoner in a chemical war.
Losing sight of the life it's been fighting for.

Slowly all strength is lost in the battle they're in.
Pulling the trigger, Satan thinks he'll win.

Mothers, fathers, sons and daughters.
Drugs holding captive, hearts slaughtered.
Empty beds and open graves,

sadly only so many will be saved.
Society judges, families turn their backs.
A life now in ruins, so far off track.
Answers are scarce, options are limited.
Truth and light somehow seem prohibited.

Needles and pipes, bottles and lines, a life up in smoke.
Meet rock bottoms where innocence chokes.

Wake up from this nightmare where those choices took place.
Leave behind the hunt, give up the chase
of decisions that cannot be erased, of an endless race.
Staring in the mirror with an unrecognizable face.

The one thing left is Gods amazing grace.

Are You In

I can remember the first time I saw your face.
The smile that infused my being with encrypted
feelings.
You kept me at an uncomfortable distance.
I didn't understand your resistance.
I could never define the fears that brewed.
The thought of never keeping you, shadowed a
part of me I had to keep from you.
Years passed without you there.
I wore a mask pretending not to care.

I had tasted the decadence of your sweet love,
only to find it wasn't mine to keep.
It slipped through my fingers.
Crushed my ability to believe in forever.

I can remember earth shattering love that I found
in your bedroom eyes.
I felt it again the other day, when you decided to
look my way.

I'm different now, as are you.
Time did its part to teach us lessons, causing us
to return to our lover's sessions.

Not out of comfort or disillusionment.
Not out of loneliness or regret, but out of
authentic and profound realization that now is
the time. Our time.

Here we have found growth, understanding,
compassion and unapologetic love that has
endured every test of time and destruction. No
obstacle has proven to win.

As I look in your eyes, my heart beats with one
question-Are you in?

The One That Got Away Came Back To Stay

You were always the one, my first choice. My rerun.
I tried every angle, fought, faded and lost my voice.
Nobody could ever compare.
I'd go against all I knew to get close to you.
The look in your eyes lit the flame.
Your touch added fuel to a fire I couldn't tame.
Our wild love is something most will never know.
A passion that runs so deep it meets me in my sleep.
Storms of destruction set out to sabotage what was real.
At times the aftermath was too much to humanly feel.
Our feet departed in opposing directions,
losing the love that was so infectious.
Pain so great but pride gave no objections.
Time and distance cannot break what is precious.
Life brings us back to the path pointed home, to harvest the seed that was positively sewn.

The same hearts with minds that have grown.
Finally aligned with understanding eyes that
know.
This love we have is where we belong.
You are my reason behind every love song.
My heart is at home inside you calloused hands.
The power in your kiss and that look in your
eyes can bring me to my knees, but now is when
I stand.
Together we stand, hand in hand.
You'll always be my man.
Storms of life can weather our bodies, but this
love endures.
It's pure and true.
The past lives behind us, let it stay.
All I can see is your face and I savor your taste.
My magic man, with powers to make me feel.

I had hardened my soul, froze my heart, love
was no deal.
But your presence brings warmth and comfort.
Your ability to soften my exterior and enter my
locked chambers is startling.
You make my heart sing.
Fight for me my love, battle this life along side
me.
Stronger together, that's why we don't say never.
Bring me out of this reverie, you are my only.

After all these years, nothing has changed, just some events rearranged.

Reflections From a Broken Past

I often wonder what you see when you look at
me.
Do you see weakness from tears I've cried or the
strength it took to wipe them away?
Do you see the fears that got in my way or the
courage I used to lead them astray?

Many nights I sang sad songs, that got me by,
but God gave me a new song that lifted me high.
He showed me that in my solitude I could not
stay.
By grace I walked through the grief to find a
brand new day.
I learned to laugh while I cry, to smile because
somehow I was getting by!
Yesterday cut like a knife, but I was willing to
TRY.

Torment thought it was here to stay,
but His light led me down a brand new way.
I am a new woman full of love for myself.
I am a mother teaching my girl to value herself.
This world can be dark, cold, and lonely.
The good news is, it's not that only.

The sun comes up and shines on life.
Everyday is a new chance because of His loving sacrifice.
Laughter is the language that mends my broken heart.
Music is the sound of healing and that's just the start.
Gratitude is the correction to my diluted perception.
I know I may stumble and fall,
but it doesn't mean I'll crumble and stay down after all.

Let Me Love You

Isolation breeds infestation of poisonous
thoughts that overkill. Mind, body, and soul;
tension builds and takes its toll. We are miles
apart, but I feel your pain. Shutting me out only
increases the strain.
Let me in my love, tell me where you've been.
Building a barrier keeps me out but locks you in.
It's a dangerous game where nobody wins.
Time has passed and we are older now.
I can love you right let me show you how.
Life is a series of trials that put love to the test.
How we respond is what sets us apart from the
rest.
As I look at my empty bed, I am curious as to
what thoughts consume your head.
It's time to let our minds align.
Comfort and understanding is what we'll find.
You don't have to do this alone.
Please my love pick up the phone.
Isolation will cause destruction.
Communication helps us function.
It's safe to come and lean on me.
I promise it's the only place I want to be.

Rest Easy

There was a time when all I could see were the memories.
Tear stained face, hemorrhaging heart.
I stayed isolated and reclusive.
I was stuck in loss.
Losing you is a pain that no words can explain.
There is no recovering from that tragic day.
There is evolving; learning to live without.
A yearn to go back, but forced to go on.
My greatest lessons were born from the the toughest battles.
Who I am now is a direct result of loving you.
Your existence and passing have had the most influential impact on breaking me down and building me back up.
For so long, anger and rage took up valuable space, until God brought me face to face.
He had to open my eyes to help me realize I had been believing too many lies.
The enemy lurks, using circumstances to bend the truth.
Pain became a convenient excuse to lash out and break the rules.
All reason left my mind during this gloomy time.

I built walls.
Going on was too impossible to try.
All I could do was cry.
Somehow a year past me by.
I found myself on the bathroom floor,
Knocking on death's sullen door.

God heard my pleading cries.
He saved me and exposed the lies.
Another chance to live.
I'd have to learn to forgive.

I wore honesty like a crown.
Tears erased.
Smiles overtook the frown.
Laughter became a frequent sound.
I lost a part of me, dealing with grief.
The part of me where you live will never die.
Only God had the power to open my eyes.
I opened His powerful book and took a much
needed look.
Answers flew off the page.
I began to understand my rage.
The healing hurt, but the pain was necessary.
I committed to complete transparency.
The more I surrendered to God, the less the
enemy could control.
He had to let go of his oppressive hold.

Chains of despair began to break.
Trusting God was a chance I had to take.

Finally released from my self-made prison.
Once again finding gratitude in things hidden.

Your existence will always be a treasure.
The love I have for you goes without measure.
I had to learn to live without your presence.
I'll never forget the lessons.
I hope when you look down you are proud of
me.
I'm becoming exactly who you wanted me to be.

Painted Picture

Crash into me like the waves of the sea.
Sun glitters across turbulent waters.
Hope floats along the surface.
Wind blows cares away.
Moon peaks behind clouds, beckoning lovers of
the night.
The sand awaits footprints to be made.
The beach hold memories of the day.
Constellations formed high above, written in the
stars promising love.
Beautiful disasters have taken place, but in this
serene scene you'd never know.
Casting eyes upon this natural canvas bring
harmony.
It's a tranquil masterpiece painted by the hands
of the Creator.
The sun sets over the horizon.
Sun kissed skin and moonlit eyes.
Brand new desires arise.
Falling in love with this peaceful moment.
Caress the mind and soothe the soul.
Magic of the ocean puts me under a spell.
Summer is ending and autumn rushes in.
Hair wisps in the wind.
Never wanting to escape the paradise we're in.

Press pause on this glorious day.
Capture the moment, nourish it to stay.
Remember love just this way.

CPSIA information can be obtained
at www.ICGtesting.com
Printed in the USA
BVHW050120060723
666779BV00016B/692